LEBANON

A CHRONICLE OF RESILIENCE

BY:

ALI R. JABER

FROM THE PERSPECTIVE OF A LEBANESE AMERICAN.

Table of Contents

Introduction

Lebanon, a country snugly situated between the breathtaking Mediterranean Sea and the sturdy peaks of the Mount Lebanon range, is similar to a living storybook filled with tales of history, culture, and challenges. It is not a big country; however, it has a lot of history to its name.

You have these stunning views of the Mediterranean Sea on one side – all blue and vast, like a giant swimming pool for the country. Then, on the other side, there are these rugged mountains, the Mount Lebanon range, standing tall and proud, like the backbone of the whole scene.

Lebanon has an old history – we are talking ancient times. It has seen civilizations come and go, like the cool kids in school changing every semester. Phoenicians, Romans, Arab Caliphates – you name it, they have left their mark inside the Lebanese territory.

Let us not get too caught up in the past, as Lebanon is still very much a thriving country today. The people of Lebanon have gone through so much, various wars and civilizations have shaped the country's identity. It has not always been easy, but the people of Lebanon have demonstrated an unbelievable spirit. They are resilient, which is a fancy way of stating they do not give up easily.

And then the economic situation comes into play. The currency took a nosedive, causing a bit of chaos.

The Lebanese people are not the ones to just throw in the towel and give up. They have found ways to keep going, navigating through the mess with a mix of creativity and determination.

Lebanon can be classified as a melting pot, but instead of soup, it is a mix of cultures, ideas, and vibes!

Now, let us focus on the heartbeat of this melting pot – Beirut, the capital. Back in the day, people called it "Paris of the Middle East." And you know what? That is not just a random compliment; it has some serious truth to it. Beirut has this vibe of sophistication and tolerance – it is like the city is saying, "*Everyone's welcome here!*"

Look at it this way, in ancient times, there was the Phoenicians – the OG sailors and traders – and they were doing their thing in Lebanon. They were the trendsetters, creating this cool, sea-loving culture that still echoes in Lebanon's coastal vibes today. Fast forward a bit, and the Romans rolled into town. You know, the toga-wearing, Colosseum-building crew. They left their architectural stamp on Lebanon, giving it this classic touch.

Then came the Arab Caliphates, bringing in a whole new flavor to the mix. Each of these civilizations contributed by practicing their traditions in Lebanon, leaving behind bits of their awesomeness. The result? A vibrant piece of history no matter where you look – we have the ancient ruins, the architecture, and the stories that were passed down through generations.

Yet, within the captivating scenery of Lebanon, there lies a story etched with profound challenges. As we embark on this exploration through the complex history of Lebanon, we confront the shadows of the past and the urgent issues of the present. The narrative unfolds against a backdrop of crisis, where persistence transforms from a mere virtue to an absolute necessity for survival.

Lebanon, despite its breathtaking landscapes, is a country that has weathered substantial challenges throughout its existence. The historical journey takes us through periods of conflicts, societal upheavals, and economic turbulence. These challenges are not distant echoes but rather integral chapters in Lebanon's story.

The pressing issues faced by the Lebanese people today form a critical part of this narrative. From economic uncertainties to political complexities, the country grapples with contemporary challenges that demand immediate attention. The journey we undertake is not a stroll through serene landscapes alone; it is a conscious acknowledgment of the multifaceted struggles that have shaped and continue to shape Lebanon.

In this narrative, crisis is not a distant concept; it is the very air that the Lebanese people breathe. Resilience, therefore, is not an optional trait but a survival skill honed through navigating the storms of adversity. It is the strength that emerges when faced with challenges that seem insurmountable.

As we immerse ourselves in Lebanon's story, it becomes clear that the call for resilience is not a romanticized idea but a pragmatic response to the complexities the nation faces. The beauty of Lebanon, while undeniable, does not overshadow the resilience required to thrive amidst difficulties. It is a place where each step forward is marked not just by the allure of the landscape but by the tenacity of a people determined to persevere in the face of crisis.

In the following pages, we delve into the annals of Lebanon's past, exploring the echoes of history that reverberate through the ages. From the enduring weight of wars to the seismic economic tremors that have shaken its foundations, Lebanon's story is one of trials and tribulations, yet combined with the remarkable spirit of its people.

Lebanon's history is marked by the weight of wars that have profoundly shaped its destiny. The impact of these conflicts spans from ancient times to the complexities of modern-day struggles. The Lebanese people have been direct witnesses to the ever-shifting dynamics in the region, each conflict leaving a lasting imprint on the nation and its inhabitants.

The legacy of ancient conflicts, including those involving the Phoenicians, Romans, and later the Arab Caliphates, has embedded a sense of endurance in the Lebanese DNA. However, it is the more recent struggles, notably the Lebanese Civil War (1975-1990) and the challenges that followed, that have left an indelible mark on the country.

The Lebanese Civil War, characterized by sectarian tensions and external interventions, tore at the very essence of the nation. The scars of that conflict are not only visible in the physical infrastructure but also in the collective memory of the Lebanese people. The aftermath brought with it the need for reconstruction, both in terms of physical infrastructure and the rebuilding of societal bonds.

Moreover, Lebanon has found itself entangled in regional conflicts, becoming a battleground for geopolitical struggles. The repercussions of these conflicts have echoed within the borders of Lebanon, evaluating the resilience of its people and shaping their responses to adversity.

Lebanon grapples with palpable economic challenges that have sent tremors through its society, leaving no corner untouched. The collapse of the currency, a profound blow to the economy, has unleashed ripples that extend into every aspect of Lebanese life. The impact is not confined to a particular group or sector; it permeates through all strata of society.

The collapse of the Lebanese currency has manifested as a stark and pervasive crisis. Its consequences are felt daily by individuals and businesses alike. The devaluation of the currency has led to skyrocketing prices, diminishing the purchasing power of the Lebanese people. Basic necessities, once taken for granted, have become a luxury for many.

The economic downturn has not spared any sector. Businesses face the challenge of navigating an environment where operational costs surge while revenues plummet. Unemployment rates rise, exacerbating the strain on families and communities. The instability in the financial system has eroded savings, and the prospect of economic recovery seems distant.

Amid this fiscal turmoil, the response from the Lebanese people is nothing short of remarkable. Their fortitude shines through as they confront adversity head-on. In the face of economic uncertainty, they have displayed resilience, adapting to the new normal with a determination to survive and thrive.

The innovative spirit of the Lebanese people becomes a beacon of hope in these trying times. Entrepreneurs explore creative solutions to sustain their businesses, and communities come together to support each other. The crisis has sparked a wave of resourcefulness, with individuals finding inventive ways to make ends meet and preserve a semblance of normalcy.

It is not just a narrative of struggle; it is a testament to the strength of a people facing economic adversity. The stories emerging from Lebanon are not just about enduring; they are about forging a path forward despite the challenges. The economic challenges may have casted a shadow, but the Lebanese people stand resilient, determined to navigate through the storm and emerge on the other side with a renewed sense of hope and possibility.

In the face of adversity, voices of protest have echoed through the streets, a manifestation of the collective frustration and yearning for change.

As we embark on this journey through Lebanon's history, our narrative strives for a neutrality that transcends political and religious divides. This is a story about the Lebanese people—their struggles, their resilience, and their unwavering spirit.

Buckle your seatbelt as we journey through the complexity of Lebanon's past and present. In the next chapters, we will peel back the layers of this country's story, exploring its struggles, celebrating its victories, and, finally, acknowledging Lebanon's tenacious strength. Welcome to **Lebanon: A chronicle of struggle and resilience**, a story that delves beyond the headlines and into the essence of a nation.

Chapter 1: Shadow of History

Long ago, way before the busy cities we see today and all the complicated things we know, Lebanon's story began. This chapter takes us back in time, looking at the start of Lebanon, the different cultures that shaped it, and the important events that created the detailed story of Lebanon's early days.

Early Roots

Lebanon's historical roots extend deep into antiquity, tracing back to a time when the Phoenicians, skilled in maritime activities and trade, played a pivotal role in shaping the foundation of what we now know as Lebanon. Their proficiency in navigation not only facilitated connections with distant lands but also laid the groundwork for a distinct culture characterized by commerce, exploration, and a way of life that was uniquely their own.

As the centuries unfolded, the region became a witness to the ebb and flow of empires. The Romans, with their grand architectural endeavors and governance, made a lasting impact on Lebanon.

The changes that happened during the Roman era stuck around and influenced how things look and feel in Lebanon till this very day. The Arab Caliphates came in later, and they added to Lebanon's way of life. They brought in a mix of traditions that were full of life and color, and these traditions have stuck around over the years, playing a big part in shaping Lebanon's identity. It is like they added new colors to the painting of Lebanon, and those colors are still there, making the whole picture richer and more vibrant. These influences are not just history; they are a part of how people in Lebanon live and see themselves.

Understanding the importance of Lebanon's history means recognizing the things that have made Lebanon what it is throughout the years. The Phoenicians were good at sailing, and this left a lasting mark on Lebanon. The Romans also left their mark with impressive skills that we can still see today. And later, the Arab Caliphates added their own traditions and way of life, creating a massive pot that is mixed with diversity.

This chapter of history is more than just a list of events that took place; it is like a story about how the people of Lebanon have stayed strong and flexible over time. It is about facing challenges and keeping that spirit alive despite the challenges. The seafaring from way back, the grand stuff the Romans did, and the traditions from the Arab Caliphates – all of this makes up the early roots of Lebanon. It is a detailed and colorful picture, showing how the people of Lebanon have been strong and determined throughout the difficulties and uncertainties.

Cultural and Geopolitical Influences:

As previously stated, Lebanon was a meeting point for various cultures due to its location in the center of the East and West. Lebanon's cultural diversity makes it a welcoming and open-minded place. Beirut, the capital, was even dubbed the "Paris of the Middle East" during its heyday as a hotspot for exchanging ideas and wonderful items.

But it is not just about being a cool meeting spot; Lebanon's location has also made it part of some sinister agendas played by powerful nations. Located between the Mediterranean Sea and the mountains, everyone wanted to have a piece of Lebanon.

Lebanon is not just a country on a map; it is a mixture of diverse cultures. All of this has played a role in shaping how things are in Lebanon today.

Historical Events Shaping the Nation:

The events that took place in the past have shaped how the country looks and how the Lebanese people see themselves. Consider the Crusades which caused significant battles that resounded through Lebanon's mountains, leaving a lasting impact on the land and its people. Subsequently, the Ottoman Empire assumed control for an extended period, contributing to Lebanon's architectural landscape with structures that endure today. The echoes of World War I reverberated in Lebanon, leading to a phase of French control, a period known as the French Mandate and this era played a crucial role in steering Lebanon towards its path to independence.

To explain this further, the Crusades marked a stormy period of conflict, and their effects were palpable in Lebanon's topography. The Ottoman rule that followed left a tangible legacy in the form of noteworthy and aesthetically pleasing structures that continue to stand as a testament to that era. World War I had a ripple effect on Lebanon, and its aftermath saw the emergence of French influence, shaping the nation's trajectory toward autonomy.

The Ottoman era was not just about governance; it significantly influenced Lebanon's architectural and sociopolitical essence too. The structures erected during this time stand as historical landmarks. Post-World War I, the French Mandate period was instrumental in paving the way for Lebanon to break free and establish itself as an independent nation.

These historical events are not faraway reflections, but important chapters in the formation of Lebanon's identity. The conflicts, the Ottoman legacy, the reverberations of World War I, and the journey to independence under French influence all add to Lebanon's rich and complicated history, which lives on in the people's collective memory.

These are not random stories; they are real events that have made Lebanon what it is today. The Crusades, the Ottoman era, World War I, and the French Mandate – have all contributed to the complex and rich identity of Lebanon, creating a history that the people carry with them.

People in Lebanon have been strong throughout the struggle and difficulties, and everyone has witnessed the resilience of the Lebanese people. As we explore Lebanon's past, we must figure out and understand the historical events that took place, we are learning about the detailed and complex history of Lebanon.

Questions

1.   Early History of Lebanon:
- What were some key aspects of Lebanon's early history that helped shape its identity?
- How did the Phoenicians contribute to Lebanon's development during ancient times?
- In what ways did early civilizations impact the culture and foundations of Lebanon?

2.   Cultural and Geopolitical Influences:
- How has Lebanon's location at the crossroads of the East and West influenced its culture over the centuries?
- Why is Beirut referred to as the "Paris of the Middle East," and what does this title signify?

- How has Lebanon been affected by being strategically positioned between the Mediterranean Sea and the mountainous hinterlands?

3. Historical Events Shaping the Nation:

- How did the Crusades leave a lasting impact on Lebanon, and what role did they play in shaping its history?

- What were the architectural contributions of the Ottoman Empire during its rule in Lebanon?

- How did World War I and the subsequent French Mandate influence Lebanon's journey towards independence?

4. General Reflection:

- In what ways do the early history, cultural influences, and historical events collectively contribute to Lebanon's unique identity?

- How has the resilience of the Lebanese people been demonstrated throughout these historical periods?

- What echoes of the past can be observed in Lebanon's present-day society and culture?

5. Personal Connection:

- How does understanding Lebanon's early history and cultural influences enhance your appreciation for its modern identity?

- Can you draw any parallels between Lebanon's historical experiences and the challenges faced by nations today?

- What aspects of Lebanon's history resonate with you on a personal level?

Chapter 2: The Weight of Wars

As we delve into the impact of these wars, we witness not only the scars left on the land but also the profound consequences felt by its people. The result of wars extends beyond the battlefield, reaching into the very crux of society and the complexities of the economy.

Impact of Wars on Lebanon:

The Lebanese Civil War (1975-1990) and conflicts with neighboring countries have left not only physical but also psychological scars on the nation. Cities, once vibrant and thriving, now lay in ruins, bearing witness to the toll exacted on Lebanon's infrastructure.

The human cost is immeasurable, with countless lives lost, families uprooted, and an entire generation marked by the trauma of conflict. The consequences extend far beyond the immediate battleground, reaching into the daily lives of individuals. Education is interrupted, healthcare services are disrupted, and a pervasive erosion of a sense of security lingers. The scars of war become an integral part of the collective memory, influencing the narratives that are handed down through generations.

■■

UN Refugee Agency Report: *Lingering Effects of the Lebanon War: Struggles with Poverty and Traumatized Children*

While the bombs may have ceased falling, the aftermath of this summer's war in Lebanon continues to haunt tens of thousands of its residents. Lives remain disrupted, economic hardship persists, and children grapple with the trauma they endured. The UN Refugee Agency (UNHCR) is actively engaged in supporting children to overcome the emotional toll of the conflict.

In discussions facilitated by UNHCR at a social development center in Chiyah, a densely populated neighborhood in southern Beirut, displaced Lebanese women shared their struggles. Many have been unable to return home since the fighting ceased, facing profound challenges, such as the loss of homes, relatives, or personal injuries.

The impact on children is particularly poignant, with some avoiding conversation, others fearful of returning home, and some refusing to venture outside. *According to Carol El Sayed*, a community services officer with UNHCR, children in certain areas of southern Beirut still discuss the sound of hovering planes and bombs, underscoring the enduring trauma.

Recognizing the depth of the ongoing problems faced by those displaced by the war, UNHCR has collaborated with the Chiyah development center to continue discussion groups and plan psycho-social activities specifically designed to help children aged eight to twelve overcome the lingering effects of the conflict.

Despite the official cessation of hostilities, the situation remains complex. At the peak of the war, around a million Lebanese fled their homes for safety, either within Lebanon, Syria, or other countries. While many returned once hostilities ceased, a significant number discovered the loss of their homes, forcing them back into temporary accommodation. Official estimates indicate that as of the beginning of this month, approximately 200,000 people remained displaced.

The economic fallout has been substantial, with increased unemployment and soaring rents due to a limited housing supply. Schools have been damaged or destroyed, placing additional financial burdens on parents already struggling to meet daily needs.

UNHCR, in collaboration with local groups and authorities, is distributing emergency items such as tents, mattresses, and blankets to those who lost belongings in the war. However, the pressing needs extend beyond immediate relief. Discussions with affected communities and the government highlight the necessity of addressing longer-term challenges, including shelter, medical services, and schooling

■■

The toll on Lebanon's infrastructure is evident in the physical remnants of destruction—

crumbling buildings, shattered streets, and landmarks that stand as evidence of the challenges faced. Beyond these visible signs, the impact is deeply personal. Families torn apart, students deprived of educational opportunities, and individuals grappling with the profound effects of living through stormy times.

When schools are shut down, students are left without education, and this could impact the lives of many. Hospitals may have a difficult time treating patients during wars, and this could cause both physical and mental health issues for civilians. Feeling safe becomes an issue, and these situations could make people feel at risk all the time.

These are not far-off tales; they are real-life situations that have molded how the Lebanese people think and feel. The marks of war are not just on buildings; they are embedded into how society works, changing how people see each other, their viewpoints, and their everyday existence. As Lebanon moves forward from the impact of wars, the strength of its people stands out as a guiding light, showing a way towards recovery and reconstruction.

Consequences on Society and Economy:

The consequences of wars in Lebanon go beyond what you can see in the physical damage.

They seep into the very structure of the Lebanese society, creating challenges for how communities come together, especially with the diverse mix of religions and ethnicities. Rebuilding trust and finding common ground becomes difficult in the aftermath, as the scars of war are profound.

■■■

Economic Dislocation and Recovery in Lebanon: Consequences of the Civil War

The economic aftermath of the prolonged Lebanese civil war from 1975 to 1990 has left indelible marks on the nation's social essence and economic landscape. This section delves into the far-reaching consequences, focusing on the economic toll, challenges to social cohesion, and the daunting task of rebuilding.

*1.	Economic Fallout:*

The direct economic cost of the civil war is measured by the loss of potential output during the conflict. Estimating the cumulative loss of output from 1975 to 1993, the figures reveal staggering consequences. The loss of output during this period is at least LL 98 billion at constant 1974 prices, equivalent to about 24 times the value of Lebanon's 1993 real GDP. The economic impact is far-reaching, affecting growth rates and per capita income.

2.   *Slow Recovery and Growth Challenges:*

Lebanon's real GDP growth, which averaged 5.8 percent annually during 1964–74, plummeted to a dismal rate of minus 2.7 percent from 1975 to 1993. Real per capita GDP witnessed a decline of 3.0 percent during this period, emphasizing the severe economic setback. The significant decline in investment, dislocation of markets, and the destruction of physical capital hampered productivity growth, hindering the nation's ability to recover swiftly.

3.   *Long Road to Reattaining Pre-War Levels*:

The analysis suggests that the road to economic recovery is prolonged. The real per capita income, reduced to about one-third of its 1974 level by the end of the 1980s, faces a slow journey back. Projections indicate that, assuming steady growth rates, Lebanon could reattain its 1974 per capita income level by the early 2000s. However, the transition from the low postwar income level to the steady state is expected to span several generations.

4.   *Convergence Dynamics:*

The concept of convergence, indicating the speed at which an economy closes the gap between its actual and steady-state incomes, provides insights into Lebanon's recovery trajectory. Various scenarios suggest that, even with optimistic assumptions, it could take decades to bridge the substantial gap created by the war. The economic growth and convergence involve a protracted transition, marked by diminishing returns to capital.

5.   *Capital Loss and Recovery Dynamics:*

The nature of capital loss during the war plays a pivotal role in shaping recovery dynamics. Lebanon, having experienced more destruction in physical capital than human capital, mirrors economies like Germany after World War II. The potential for a faster recovery exists, especially with continued political and economic stability.

In conclusion, the economic consequences of the civil war in Lebanon are profound, encompassing a slow recovery, challenges to growth, and a complex journey towards reattaining pre-war economic levels. The interplay between the loss of physical and human capital, coupled with the dynamics of convergence, underscores the intricate path ahead for Lebanon's economic revival[1].

---

[1] **II. Economic Ramifications of the Civil War*: Authors*: Jose Martelino, S. Nuri Erbas, Adnan Mazarei, Sena Eken, Paul Cashin

On the economic front, Lebanon faces a heavy financial burden due to the costs of reconstruction after wars. This strain on resources hampers the country's ability to focus on development. The repetitive cycles of conflict not only stall economic growth but also worsen issues like poverty and unemployment. Businesses grapple with the challenges of operating in an uncertain and unstable environment.

Resilience in the Middle of Conflict:

In the face of the profound challenges posed by wars, the tenacity of the Lebanese people stands out. Their resilience serves as a powerful testament to the indomitable nature of the human spirit. Despite the adversities brought about by conflict, communities unite to offer mutual support, engaging in the reconstruction of homes, schools, and the restoration of cultural landmarks. The Lebanese diaspora, too, plays a pivotal role by contributing not just financially but also by nurturing relationships that extend across borders.

Within this narrative of resilience, individual stories come to the forefront. Entrepreneurs breathe new life into businesses, educators rebuild the foundations of education, and the arts emerge as a compelling expression of resilience, providing a medium for healing and renewal. The Lebanese people, sharing a history marred by conflict, draw strength from their collective solidarity, embodying a steadfast determination to transcend the challenges they face.

That said, in facing the difficulties of wars, Lebanon's story turns into a victory over tough times. It is not just about fixing buildings but also about rebuilding the core of the nation. Even though scars linger, there is a strong spirit that will not let the challenges of the past be the only defining factor. When we dig into how wars affect Lebanon, we discover a resilience that becomes a crucial part of the nation's identity.

This resilience is not just about bouncing back; it is about becoming stronger despite hardships. Lebanon's people not only rebuild physical structures but also revive the spirit and soul of their nation. The impact of wars is not just about destruction; it is also about the incredible strength that emerges in response. The story of Lebanon is one of standing tall, rebuilding not just what is broken but also shaping a stronger identity through it all.

Questions

1.   Impact of Wars on Lebanon:

- How have wars affected the physical landscape of Lebanon?

- In what ways has the impact of wars shaped the lives of Lebanese citizens?

- Can you elaborate on specific events or periods that had a profound influence on Lebanon due to wars?

2.   Consequences on Society and Economy:

- What social changes can be observed because of wars in Lebanon?

- How have the various conflicts influenced the economy of Lebanon?

- Are there particular sectors or aspects of society that have experienced more pronounced consequences?

3. Resilience Amidst Conflict:

- Can you provide examples of resilience demonstrated by the Lebanese people during times of conflict?

- How has the concept of resilience evolved in Lebanon's societal and cultural context?

- In what ways has resilience played a role in rebuilding both society and the economy after periods of conflict?

Chapter 3: The Economic Tremors

The Cause of its Economic Woes

Lebanon's economy is like a complicated puzzle showing many challenges that have strongly affected the country. As we investigate this issue, we are moving through a landscape formed by a mix of events happening inside and outside of the country.

Historical Backdrop:

Delving into Lebanon's economic challenges requires us to reflect on its historical journey. This path, characterized by moments of prosperity and upheaval, has been significantly shaped by geopolitical forces, conflicts, and changes in worldwide economic patterns.

Over the years, Lebanon's economic landscape has not evolved in isolation but rather in response to broader global events and regional dynamics. Geopolitical factors, such as its strategic location in the Middle East, have played a pivotal role. The nation's history bears witness to both periods of economic growth and disruptions triggered by conflicts.

Lebanon has shown resilience and adaptability over time, dealing with ups and downs in its history. Knowing this history is crucial to understanding today's economic challenges. It is like uncovering a story where economic struggles are woven into bigger global and regional events, creating a complex and detailed picture.

Structural Weaknesses

Lebanon's economic foundation relies heavily on its institutions and policies, acting as essential pillars for sustained growth. Unfortunately, these crucial elements have faced significant challenges. Inefficiencies, corruption, and a lack of strong governance have left deep marks on the system. The impact of these structural weaknesses extends across different sectors, creating obstacles that hinder the country's ability to achieve lasting and meaningful economic development.

In terms of inefficiencies, bureaucratic processes and administrative hurdles slow down economic activities, making it harder for businesses to operate smoothly. Corruption further exacerbates the situation, siphoning off resources and fostering an environment where fair competition struggles to thrive. This not only distorts the economic playing field but also undermines the trust that both domestic and international investors place in Lebanon's economic institutions.

The absence of robust governance compounds these issues, as the regulatory frameworks and oversight mechanisms fall short of ensuring accountability and transparency. Without effective governance, there is a higher likelihood of mismanagement and misuse of resources, hindering the efficient allocation of funds towards projects and initiatives that could spur economic growth.

These structural weaknesses have a cascading effect on various sectors. In the financial realm, the banking sector, once considered a cornerstone of Lebanon's economy, faces challenges due to inadequate regulations and supervision. This has contributed to financial instability, affecting the confidence of depositors and investors.

Similarly, the industrial and manufacturing sectors struggle to reach their full potential, grappling with bureaucratic hurdles and an uneven playing field. This not only stifles innovation and competitiveness but also limits the sectors' contribution to the overall economic output.

Agriculture, another crucial component of Lebanon's economy, faces challenges related to land tenure issues, outdated farming practices, and a lack of modernization. These factors impede the sector's ability to thrive, impacting both rural livelihoods and the country's food security.

Addressing these structural weaknesses requires comprehensive reforms in institutions, policies, and governance. It necessitates a commitment to transparency, accountability, and the rule of law. Only through such transformative measures can Lebanon hope to overcome these challenges and build a more resilient and sustainable economic future.

Public Debt Quagmire:

Lebanon confronts a daunting challenge, grappling with the complexities of a rapidly expanding public debt—a quagmire that threatens the very foundations of its economic stability. The roots of this burgeoning debt crisis delve into a complex interplay of fiscal policies, political choices, and external pressures, weaving a narrative that demands a detailed understanding.

The genesis of Lebanon's public debt predicament can be traced to fiscal policies that, over time, led to persistent budget deficits. The government's decision to finance these deficits through borrowing created a snowball effect, contributing to the escalation of the country's overall debt burden. Political considerations, often combined with economic decisions, further exacerbated the situation, leading to a fiscal landscape fraught with challenges.

External pressures, including global economic dynamics and regional conflicts, also played a role in shaping Lebanon's debt trajectory. The country's vulnerability to external shocks, combined with a reliance on foreign aid, has left it exposed to the whims of the international economic climate. As global conditions fluctuate, Lebanon finds itself navigating turbulent waters, with repercussions reverberating through its fiscal corridors.

Addressing the public debt quagmire demands a delicate equilibrium between fiscal prudence and socio-economic considerations. Austerity measures, while essential for restoring fiscal discipline, must be implemented judiciously to avoid exacerbating social inequalities. Simultaneously, efforts to enhance revenue generation, through tax reforms and efficient resource allocation, can contribute to a sustainable fiscal path.

Comprehensive reforms are imperative to tackle the structural issues underpinning Lebanon's fiscal challenges. This includes reevaluating public spending, enhancing the efficiency of government institutions, and fostering an environment conducive to economic growth. International cooperation and support are also pivotal, as Lebanon seeks to navigate the complex web of its public debt crisis and embark on a journey towards fiscal resolution.

In essence, the resolution of Lebanon's public debt quandary necessitates a multifaceted approach that addresses both the root causes and the socio-economic impact. Striking a delicate balance between fiscal responsibility and the well-being of the population is paramount for charting a course toward a more stable and sustainable economic future.

Currency Crisis:

The undulating fluctuations in the Lebanese pound transcend mere numerical values, casting profound repercussions on businesses, consumers, and the complex web of the overall economic ecosystem. To unravel the complexities of this crisis, one must delve into the intricate interplay of multifaceted factors that form its bedrock.

At the heart of Lebanon's currency crisis lie the complex threads of monetary policies, woven into the economic essence over time. The nation's monetary framework, while once stable, has encountered formidable challenges. A confluence of factors, including mismanagement, inflationary pressures, and a precarious balance between domestic and external economic forces, has contributed to the erosion of the Lebanese pound's value.

The specter of external debt looms large in the narrative of Lebanon's currency crisis. The country's dependence on foreign borrowings, often driven by the need to finance budget deficits, has created a delicate dance with international financial markets. As global economic dynamics shift, Lebanon finds itself vulnerable to the ripples of uncertainty, with the fluctuations in external debt playing a pivotal role in shaping the direction of its currency's value.

Global economic dynamics further amplify the intricacies of Lebanon's currency crisis. The nation, intricately connected to the international economic ecosystem, becomes susceptible to the ebb and flow of global financial tides. External shocks, geopolitical events, and fluctuations in commodity prices all conspire to create a volatile environment, where the fate of the Lebanese pound hangs in the balance.

Navigating the maze of Lebanon's currency crisis demands a comprehensive understanding of these interconnected factors. A strategic recalibration of monetary policies, coupled with efforts to address structural weaknesses and reduce reliance on external borrowings, becomes imperative. Fostering financial stability requires a delicate balance between domestic economic priorities and the demands of the international financial landscape.

As Lebanon grapples with the far-reaching consequences of its currency crisis, the path to economic recovery necessitates not only addressing immediate challenges but also laying the groundwork for an adaptive monetary framework. Moving forward means sorting out the complicated problems that connect the Lebanese pound to the overall economy. The goal is to bring back stability, confidence, and continuous growth.

Impact on Businesses and Employment:

The challenges in Lebanon have had a significant impact on businesses, which are crucial for any economy. These economic issues have caused problems for businesses, affecting how well they can survive and thrive. This, in turn, has led to difficulties in employment, as job markets are dealing with the consequences of these economic shocks.

Lebanon's businesses are facing disruptions that make it harder for them to operate smoothly. These disruptions can include things like supply chain issues, financial instability, and decreased consumer spending. When businesses struggle, it has a ripple effect on the job market. Companies may have to cut back on hiring, and in some cases, they may even need to lay off workers.

For the individuals who depend on these jobs, it creates a challenging situation. Finding new employment becomes more difficult, and those who are employed may face uncertainties about the stability of their positions. This economic instability puts pressure on the entire employment ecosystem.

Additionally, businesses play a vital role in contributing to the overall economic health of a nation. They generate revenue, pay taxes, and contribute to the growth of the economy. When businesses face challenges, it affects the larger economic landscape.

To address these issues, it's crucial to implement strategies that support businesses, such as providing financial assistance, creating a stable economic environment, and fostering conditions for growth. By doing so, not only can the business sector recover, but the positive impact can extend to the broader community, helping to stabilize employment and contribute to economic resilience.

External Pressures:

Lebanon's economic struggles are not happening in a vacuum; they are connected to larger global economic changes and regional factors. Understanding these factors is crucial to unravel the complexities of Lebanon's economic situation.

Geopolitical tensions, which are conflicts and issues between different countries or regions, play a role in shaping Lebanon's economic challenges. When there are tensions between nations, it can impact trade, create uncertainty, and influence investor confidence. Lebanon, being part of the global community, is inevitably affected by these geopolitical dynamics.

Trade dynamics, or the way countries engage in buying and selling goods and services, also influence Lebanon's economic landscape. Changes in global trade patterns, tariffs, and international economic policies can have direct consequences on Lebanon's ability to trade with other nations. This, in turn, affects the country's economic stability and growth.

External dependencies refer to Lebanon's reliance on other countries or international institutions for support or resources. If Lebanon is heavily dependent on external aid or subject to economic conditions set by other nations, it can limit its economic independence and decision-making.

All these factors combined, create a complex web of challenges for Lebanon's economy. To address these issues effectively, it's essential to consider not only local policies but also navigate the broader international context. Building economic resilience requires a strategic approach that takes into account both internal and external factors, fostering a balance that can withstand the pressures of a rapidly changing global economy.

Historical Economic Context: A Brief to Its Timeline

Let's trace the evolution of Lebanon's economy over time.

Era of Early Prosperity:

Lebanon boasts a rich history of economic prosperity dating back to ancient times. The region's strategic location facilitated trade routes, turning it into a hub for commerce. The Phoenicians, who inhabited the area, were renowned traders, contributing to the flourishing economy. Throughout history, Lebanon's economic landscape has been shaped by its geographical position and the entrepreneurial spirit of its people.

Impact of Conflicts:

However, Lebanon's economic trajectory has not been without disruptions. Periods of conflict and external invasions have left lasting imprints on the economy. Wars and geopolitical tensions have, at times, hindered economic growth and stability, creating challenges that the nation had to navigate.

Banking Hub of the Middle East:

In the 20th century, Lebanon emerged as a banking and financial center in the Middle East. The country's banking sector played a pivotal role, attracting deposits and investments from the region and beyond. The Lebanese Pound, pegged to the U.S. Dollar, provided stability and confidence in financial transactions.

Civil War and Economic Setbacks:

The Lebanese Civil War (1975-1990) had profound economic consequences. Infrastructure was heavily damaged, and the economy faced significant setbacks. The post-war period saw efforts to rebuild, with the Lebanese people displaying remarkable resilience. However, the scars of the conflict lingered, impacting the country's economic landscape.

Globalization and Challenges:

As the world entered an era of globalization, Lebanon faced both opportunities and challenges. Integration into the global economy brought economic benefits, but it also exposed the nation to external shocks. The interconnected nature of economies meant that global economic shifts could have a direct impact on Lebanon's economic stability.

Tourism and Services Sector:

Lebanon's services sector, particularly tourism, played a crucial role in its economy. The country's diverse cultural heritage and scenic landscapes attracted visitors from around the world. However, geopolitical events and security concerns have, at times, affected tourism, impacting an essential component of the economy.

Contemporary Economic Dynamics:

In recent decades, Lebanon has grappled with a complex economic landscape marked by a combination of internal and external factors. Issues such as public debt, structural weaknesses, and political challenges have posed significant hurdles. Navigating these challenges requires a nuanced understanding of Lebanon's historical economic context, as it provides insights into the nation's strengths, vulnerabilities, and adaptive capacities.

Understanding Lebanon's economic history is akin to unfolding a story with chapters of growth, resilience, and challenges. It is a narrative that continues to evolve, shaped by historical forces and present-day dynamics. As Lebanon seeks to address its economic complexities, a holistic perspective that considers its historical journey becomes indispensable.

Questions

1.   What is the focus of Chapter 3 - Economic Tremors?

2.   Can you provide an overview of the economic challenges discussed in this chapter?

3. What factors are identified as contributors to economic instability in the exploration of Economic Tremors?

4. Is there a historical context provided for the economic challenges faced by Lebanon?

5. How does the chapter delve into the economic landscape of Lebanon, and what insights are gained regarding its stability?

6. Are there specific events or periods highlighted that significantly impacted Lebanon's economy?

7. In what ways does the chapter connect economic challenges to broader themes within the narrative of Lebanon's journey?

8. Are there lessons or takeaways presented in this chapter regarding economic resilience or coping strategies?

9. Can you elaborate on any case studies or examples that illustrate the economic tremors discussed in this chapter?

10. How does the economic aspect interplay with other elements of Lebanon's story, such as cultural identity and community resilience?

Chapter 4: Voices of Protest

When exploring Lebanon's recent history, we find a powerful story in the chapter called "Voices of Protest." This story reflects the feelings of a frustrated public. Let us dive into this journey to learn about the social and political movements, how people express their dissatisfaction, and the important role that protests play in shaping Lebanon's current story.

Social and Political Movements:

In recent years, Lebanon, with its diverse communities and sects, has experienced a notable increase in social and political movements. These movements, fueled by a strong desire for change and reform, have emerged as influential players in shaping the country. They cover a wide range of subjects, addressing everything from economic challenges to the call for greater political accountability.

One key aspect of these movements is their dynamism, adapting to the evolving needs and concerns of the Lebanese people. Economic grievances, stemming from challenges like unemployment and financial instability, have been central to the discourse. The movements aim to address these issues, seeking solutions that can lead to a more prosperous and stable future.

Additionally, demands for political accountability resonate strongly within these movements. Citizens are voicing their concerns about the transparency and effectiveness of governance, pushing for a system that is responsive to the needs of the people. This multifaceted approach reflects the complexity of Lebanon's socio-political landscape and the relationship of various issues affecting its population.

Lebanon has diverse groups of people, and they all join these movements. Even though they come from various backgrounds, they work together for the same reasons. This shows that, despite their differences, they all want good things to happen and do not let their different beliefs get in the way.

As these movements become stronger, people in Lebanon are taking an active part in making decisions about their country. They are showing strength in dealing with difficulties. The path to real change is not just about fixing urgent problems but also about creating a shared dream for a fair, equal, and successful Lebanon.

■■■

Political Participation in Lebanon: Understanding Emerging Movements by Meray Meddah, LSE.

Meray Maddah, a Research Assistant in SIPRI's Middle East and North Africa Program, delves into Lebanon's recent political landscape in her article "*Political Participation in Lebanon: A Look into Emerging Political Movements.*" The piece provides insights into the challenges faced by the country, particularly in the aftermath of the 17 October protest movement in 2019.

Lebanon has experienced turbulent years, and the 2019 protests marked a significant turning point. The demonstrations questioned the confessional system and the long-standing political elite. New faces emerged, creating a space for previously unheard voices. Subsequently, emerging political movements (EPMs) with shared objectives formed, challenging the established ethnosectarian system. The decaying post-war political order entrenched by elites remains a hurdle, prompting the question of whether EPMs can reshape Lebanon's political landscape.

The upcoming parliamentary and municipal elections in May 2022 offer hope for change, but challenges persist. The existing electoral laws, controlled by the entrenched elites, may hinder meaningful transformation. EPMs aim to challenge this status quo, emphasizing economic and political reforms.

Several EPMs, such as Lihaqqi and Minteshreen, have distinct missions. Lihaqqi focuses on economic equality and social justice at the local level through participatory methods. On the other hand, Minteshreen, a youth-led movement, advocates for a civil state governed by the rule of law and targets the diaspora through social media outreach.

The article discusses the complex alliances, such as the Lebanese Social Democratic Party aligning with EPMs, and the challenges they may pose. The 17 October movement, catalyzed by the Beirut blast, has set the stage for EPMs, with organisations like Kulluna Irada playing a role in raising awareness on public issues.

As the elections approach, EPMs face obstacles, including contested electoral laws and elites reluctant to relinquish power. The article emphasizes the need for EPMs to run on organized platforms with clear strategies, especially given the influence of sectarian divisions in Lebanon's political system. While fundamental change may take time, the organized nature of these movements offers hope for a more structured opposition.

In conclusion, Maddah highlights the fuel crisis, electricity shortages, and the overall economic woes faced by the population. Despite the challenges, EPMs present a more organized front than previous movements, paving the way for potential political change in Lebanon.

Expression of Public Dissatisfaction:

The streets of Lebanon have transformed into a platform where people express their dissatisfaction with the way things are. Citizens from different backgrounds, feeling disillusioned with the existing situation, have come together in protests. These gatherings have provided a collective voice to individuals from all walks of life.

The reasons behind this public discontent are rooted in various issues. Economic inequality, corruption, and insufficient public services have fueled the dissatisfaction among the people. These concerns have motivated individuals to articulate their grievances in a compelling and public manner.

Picture the scenes on the streets where people, united by a common frustration, voice their concerns. It is a powerful sight as individuals from diverse backgrounds come together, demanding change and expressing their collective dissatisfaction. The protests serve as a visible and impactful way for the people of Lebanon to make their voices heard and demand a better future.

The Role of Protests in Lebanon's Present Status

Protests have become a vital part of Lebanon's modern story. They go beyond merely reacting to particular events; instead, they embody a larger plea for fundamental change.

The issues brought forward in these protests often go beyond immediate problems, showing desire for a political system that is more inclusive and accountable.

Envision a scene from one of these protests in Lebanon: people from all walks of life congregating in a single spot to demand change. *Let us concentrate on one specific demonstration.*

In a bustling square in Beirut, citizens gathered, carrying signs that echoed their shared frustrations. A young student, Nour, spoke passionately about the need for educational reforms. She expressed concern about the challenges students faced and the impact on their future. Nour's story resonated with many, creating a ripple effect of support.

As the crowd grew, diverse voices joined in, each highlighting a different aspect of the broader issues. Workers talked about economic struggles, artists emphasized the need for cultural revitalization, and families called for improved public services.

This protest was not just a reaction to a single incident; it was a collective expression of the people's aspirations for a better Lebanon. The demands went beyond immediate concerns, reflecting a shared yearning for a political system that truly represents and serves the interests of the diverse Lebanese population. The protest became a symbol of unity, a call for change echoing through the streets of Beirut and beyond.

Key Moments of Protest:

Lebanon has seen pivotal moments of protest that echoed far beyond its borders. One of these significant moments was the "***You Stink***" movement in 2015, sparked by the garbage crisis. The streets were filled with people, frustrated, and determined, coming together to demand change. This movement served as a turning point, highlighting the power of public mobilization.

Following this, in 2019, more waves of protests swept across the nation. These were not isolated events but expressions of deep-seated public frustration.

■■■

Beirut's "You Stink" Movement: Holding Officials Accountable with a Touch of Humor

Beirut's streets, formerly known as the "Paris of the Middle East," were converted into an open landfill in the summer of 2015. Corruption among authorities had long hampered solid waste management. The dilemma reached a climax when health difficulties prompted the closure of Lebanon's largest dump, causing concerned campaigners to protest. They brilliantly dubbed their ad "Talaeat Ryhatukum," which translates to "You Stink" in English.

The brilliance of this slogan lay in its play on words. In Arabic, the word for corruption, Fassad, is the same term used for spoiled, bad-smelling food. This witty title resonated with the public, and over 20,000 Lebanese took to the streets within days.

Banners reinforced the link between the garbage crisis and political corruption. One displayed photos of allegedly corrupt politicians with the header, "SOME TRASH SHOULD NOT BE RECYCLED." Another urged to "CLEAN UP THE TRASH IN THE PARLIAMENT." Remarkably, this movement broke the sectarian mold of Lebanese politics, becoming the nation's first non-sectarian movement in decades.

Although the campaign was short-lived and lacked clear demands, its accessible language paved the way for mass mobilization. The government implemented unsustainable measures to temporarily address the trash problem, but the You Stink movement of 2015 laid the groundwork for nationwide anti-corruption protests in 2019.

The campaign's legacy lives on, demonstrating how a lighthearted tagline can generate a serious call to accountability. The simplicity and comedy of "You Stink" sparked bigger discussions about corruption that echoed well beyond Lebanon's borders.

Youth Engagement and Digital Activism:

Lebanon's protests have a standout feature—the energetic involvement of young people and the influence of digital activism. The youth actively use social media platforms to fuel the momentum, swiftly spreading information and creating a hub for various voices to come together. These tech-savvy youngsters are crucial in magnifying the protests' effects and attracting global attention.

Young individuals, armed with smartphones and a passion for change, take to platforms like Facebook, Instagram, and Twitter. They share updates, videos, and stories, creating a digital wave that resonates with people locally and globally. This is not just about hashtags and trending topics; it is about a generation leveraging technology to make their voices heard.

In the very the heart of Lebanon, a movement unfolds online and offline. Young activists organize gatherings, share real-time updates, and build a sense of unity through digital channels. They transcend geographical boundaries, connecting with the diaspora and the international community. It is evidence for the power of the youth and the digital age colliding to drive social change.

The impact is profound. The world watches as these youth-driven movements unfold, understanding that the future is inextricably linked to the aspirations of the young. Digital activism is not just a tool; it is a megaphone for a generation demanding change. Through pixels/images and protests, the youth of Lebanon etch their narrative onto the global stage.

Challenges and Achievements:

Lebanon's protests, though impactful, grapple with challenges that evaluate their resilience. As enthusiastic voices rise, so do obstacles like repression, political divides, and the intricate nature of tackling deep-seated issues. Yet, within this tug-of-war between aspirations and adversities, these movements have achieved a remarkable feat.

People from different social classes, united by shared grievances, step into the public sphere. They bring attention to issues that have long lingered in the shadows – economic disparities, corruption, and inadequate services. However, as they raise their collective voice, they encounter resistance. Authorities may respond with measures to stifle dissent, and political differences among the protesters themselves may emerge.

These challenges, while daunting, do not diminish the significance of what is being achieved. The protests spark a flame of civic engagement that refuses to be extinguished. In the face of adversity, individuals find common ground, fostering a sense of unity that transcends divisions. It is a poignant reminder that the journey toward change is seldom a smooth one.

As the world watches Lebanon's struggle for a reimagined socio-political landscape, there is a realization that the impact of these protests extends beyond immediate policy changes. They plant seeds of awareness, urging a reevaluation of Lebanon's collective priorities. The achievements may not be instant, but the transformation they inspire is a testament to the power of collective voices shaping the future of a nation.

Towards Reform and Renewal:

In Lebanon, a collective voice has risen in protest, echoing the shared desire for transformative reforms and a renewed governance system. The call for change encompasses a demand for greater transparency and accountability from the country's leadership.

The path from expressing discontent to achieving substantial transformations is undeniably challenging, reminiscent of casting stones into a pond, generating ripples that hold the potential to redefine Lebanon's overall direction.

These protests signify a multidimensional movement, where individuals from diverse backgrounds converge in a shared aspiration for a more just and equitable society. The participants articulate a demand for systemic shifts, challenging traditional power structures and advocating for responsive governance. The challenges on this journey are formidable, yet the resilience of the protestors, representing a spectrum of activists and citizens, suggests a commitment to pushing the boundaries of the status quo.

The essence of these protests lies in their role as agents of change, pushing the boundaries of conventional governance and fostering a collective push towards a more inclusive and responsive political landscape. The metaphorical stones cast into the water symbolize the far-reaching impact of these collective voices, creating concentric ripples that extend beyond the immediate protests, with the potential to reshape Lebanon's socio-political course.

As the protesters persist in challenging entrenched norms and demanding a government attuned to the needs of its people, they contribute to a broader narrative of societal evolution. The echoes of these protests serve as a potent force, resonating with the aspirations of citizens who envision a Lebanon that reflects their collective values, aspirations, and hopes for the future. While the path to tangible change remains demanding, the enduring echoes of these protests offer a glimpse into a potential new direction for Lebanon – one characterized by responsiveness, accountability, and a genuine commitment to the welfare of its diverse population.

To sum it up, the "Voices of Protest" in Lebanon represent the hopes and frustrations of many different people. They show a desire for a fair and equal society, giving us a way to see how the country and its people are changing.

Questions

1.   Can you provide a summary of the social and political movements discussed in this chapter?

2.   How does the chapter explore the expression of public dissatisfaction within the context of Lebanon's story?

3.   What role do protests play in shaping Lebanon's narrative, as highlighted in this chapter?

4.   Are there specific instances or events of protests that are emphasized in the narrative?

5.   In what ways does the chapter analyze the impact of public voices and activism on Lebanon's socio-political landscape?

6.   Are there connections made between the Voices of Protest and other elements, such as economic challenges or cultural identity, within Lebanon's journey?

7.   Does the chapter provide insights into the outcomes or consequences of the protests discussed?

8.   How are the Voices of Protest portrayed in relation to the resilience theme woven throughout the story?

9.   Can you elaborate on any personal stories or testimonials that illustrate the experiences of individuals involved in the protests mentioned in this chapter?

Chapter 5: Human Stories Amidst the Rubble

After a crisis, among the damaged buildings and chaos, there are stories of people being strong and facing difficulties. These are stories of how people keep going even when things are tough. In this chapter, we will hear from Lebanese people who have gone through challenging times, both in their lives and from big events. Their stories help us see the human part of struggling, the strong spirit that does not give up even when situations become difficult.

Getting Back Up

Lebanon, a country with a lot of history, culture, and diversity, has faced many demanding situations. Real stories come from the people of this resilient country. These stories tell us about their strength, determination, and the powerful desire to rebuild the country.

The Echoes of Beirut: Rebuilding from the Blast

On August 4th, 2020, Lebanon faced an inconvenient situation. There was a huge explosion in Beirut that destroyed parts of the city and damaged several buildings. The people of Beirut had to deal with the aftermath and damage immediately after the explosion.

Rana's Story:

Rana, a resident of Beirut states that her world turned upside down when the blast hit her apartment. As she talks about that scary day, the fear comes back in her words. "The sound was like nothing I've ever heard, and the force threw me across the room. My windows broke, and the whole city was covered in a thick cloud of smoke and dust," she shares, her voice shaking with the memory.

In the next weeks, Rana, along with many others, had the hard job of building everything again. The damage in the city was like the deep hurt in its people. "It was a lot, but we couldn't stay down. We needed to build not just our homes but our lives again," As Rana reflects on the events her eyes show the strength that comes from having no other choice.

While fixing things up, Rana met Samir, an old man with a lot of memories in the lines on his face. Their talk was more than just sad stories. Samir, touching a saved picture, told of a time when the neighborhood was full of joy. "This was my daughter's wedding picture. The happiness from that day feels like a faraway dream now," he sighed. Rana, feeling the weight of lost happiness, gave his shoulder a comforting squeeze.

Down the damaged street, Rana found Leila, a mom going through what was left of her cozy home. Leila's eyes, tired but determined, saw Rana, making a silent connection. In the mess of damage, their shared understanding became a source of power.

In the open space, talk mixed with the noise of building. Ahmed, a young dad, shared plans for a simple playground for the neighborhood kids. "They've lost too much innocence already; we need to give them a place to just be kids," he said, with his eyes showing a promise to build more than just buildings.

Tears fell, but so did words of hope. In the middle of the mess, Rana, Samir, Leila, and Ahmed became friends. "We held each other up," Rana remembers, thinking about evenings when the open space became a meeting spot.

"There were times when I felt like giving up, but we had to keep moving. The city needed us to build again, to go against what seemed impossible," she shares.

The Beirut explosion

He is broken. He tells us how, for the first time, he now wants his children to leave Lebanon – despite having put them through the best education to stay here. Nothing compared with this – not the years of civil war, assassinations, car bombs – this was different. It is different.

We have all been affected, he tells us. Family died, friends died, homes were blown up and businesses lost.

A sudden, violent blast that sucked the oxygen out of this city and its people.

It has left many gasping for air.

"It came into our homes and took our happiness, our souls," another woman tells us. She lost her husband in the blast.

She was in the living room, he was in the kitchen. She still does not comprehend how she was unscathed, and he never made it.

"In a few seconds, I lost everything I did in my life, my house, my business. But all that can be fixed – but my love? For what? For nothing?"

The shops and restaurants are shuttered. Hamra, Mar Mikhail, Gemayzee – the few businesses that survived the economic crisis now blown to pieces.

'Everything is gone'

A Lebanese friend, who had just returned after the explosion told me how depressed he was – he is of the civil war generation.

"Everything is gone – places, even people. There is nothing to be attached to any more."

Many feel that way. They have lost family, friends, homes, businesses. Everyone has a story. Few people have much hope right now.

We visit a hospital where a forensic doctor has been busy identifying the bodies of those killed in the explosion. We discuss what state the bodies are in, what he has seen – how he feels.

"I'm taking it badly," he tells us.

"We were already struggling with corona," he says, "and the economical situation, the political situation, too many things. This is very stressful for the Lebanese people – and then this explosion came."

Providing meals for Beirut blast victims

While we talk to him, bodies are carried back and forth behind us. One wrapped in black, one in white sheeting, and basic coffins.

Death hangs in the air.

He continues: "I think, until now, there is no real reaction. What you see is a stupor, people are still in stupor regarding their dead, regarding the country, regarding what is happening. And probably they are under stress syndrome, post-trauma stress syndrome – that will take some time, one year to appear."

He tells us that usually when there is an explosion in Lebanon, people rush to hospital emergency rooms – mobbing them and they have to hire security to be able to do their jobs.

"Yes they came, of course – but they stayed outside by themselves. It's as if they wanted to know the truth – but at the same time they didn't."

'Feeling emptiness'

Denial or shock. The magnitude of what has happened here is difficult to comprehend.

Saleem is a diving instructor. He volunteered with the rescue in the early days. I ask him how he felt when he first approached the port from the sea, heading to look for survivors.

"I think the real feeling was…" he pauses to think of the right word. "The real feeling was emptiness, seeing all this."

It was chaos in these early days – and the visibility in the crater was zero … They had to feel their way with their hands.

He contemplates the bigger picture. He, like many of his generation – fought in the civil war and is no stranger to violence, to death, to political chaos.

"What happened is very big."

He too tells us that this is bigger than anything ever before.

"You know you have the capital of a country that is totally destroyed. I don't know how many years we need. You know Lebanon is passing through an economic situation that is very hard. We have problems with the international bank, and we have problems with the exchange rate, and 60-70 percent of people are not working, nobody can eat, salaries are bad, we have to deal with corona, and we have the revolution. And now we have this?"

"Will Beirut recover?" I ask him.

"Yes, the buildings will recover. The people I don't know. If they stay – maybe in like 20, 30, 40 years – because if you make a small calculation, nobody really recovered from the war of '75 yet. If they are still living, and nobody recovered from the war of the '80s and '90s, and 2006. It's hidden somewhere, you just need like a click and it will pop up. I don't think it will be easy to recover. This is a big thing. It's a big thing."

'I blame the whole state'

But there is strength. And there is humor. And there is incredible solidarity between people coming together to help each other.

Feeding each other, providing shelter, patching up this shattered city. Any real official help on the ground has been notably absent.

We interview a family who is still waiting for news of their husband, their father, more than two weeks on. He worked at the silos and was in the operation room at the time of the blast.

After speaking to his wife and his son, we finish filming. I talk to his daughter. She is 19, so eloquent, smart, and beautiful.

I tell her how amazingly strong she is and how I do not think I would have been able to keep it together if it were me in this situation.

She tells me she used to think that she could not either, but it is different when it happens to you, she says. You find the strength.

Later that night, the family gets word that their father and husband was identified.

"I blame the whole state, I blame the politicians," his wife told us earlier.

Lebanon's government resigns after Beirut blast

We attend the funeral. It is unbearably sad. His elderly mother strokes his coffin, her face creased in pain.

We can see a picture of him on her chest, held in place by her jacket. Close to her heart. No mother should have to bury their child.

His son wants an independent investigation, he wants answers.

He stands stoic but his eyes burn with pain, as his mother and sisters shake with grief.

Many here say they want answers, but in the same breath, they add they believe the truth of what happened will never come out.

Justice is another thing they question. Most people we speak to blame the entire system.

They say the explosion was the ultimate, incomprehensible symbol of decades of mismanagement, corruption and negligence – of power in the hands of a few – and admit it will be very difficult to change.

SOURCE: AL JAZEERA NEWS

Stories of Financial Strain

After the big explosion, Lebanon had another issue – the currency was collapsing, and jobs started disappearing.

In the bustling city, there is Sami, a small business owner, sharing a story of drastic change. "I poured my heart into building my business, but then this money problem hit us like a giant wave. The money lost its value, prices shot up, and many businesses had to shut down," he explains with a heavy sigh.

As Sami narrates his struggles, we meet Aisha, a fellow business owner, nodding in understanding. "It's been a tough journey," Aisha empathizes, her eyes reflecting shared hardships. "We've had to make heartbreaking choices, saying goodbye to our team, who felt like family. The burden of responsibility weighed heavily on us," Sami adds, glancing at Aisha, knowing she faced similar dilemmas.

During the country's monetary crisis, their experiences blend with those of countless business owners. The previously bustling streets now ring with talks of survival. "Every day was a struggle to keep our businesses running," Sami says, the same emotion echoing with others. Faces in the throng nod in support, recognizing the communal fight.

Sami's journey mirrors the broader challenges faced by small business owners in Lebanon. The hustle and bustle of city life now carries an air of doubts. As he reflects on the daily battles, Aisha chimes in, "We had to adapt, innovate, and sometimes it felt like we were barely holding on. But giving up wasn't an option."

The Refugee Perspective

The Syrian conflict, ongoing since 2011, has had severe consequences, resulting in the death of over 250,000 civilians and widespread destruction in Syria. The conflict has forced millions of Syrians to leave their homes, either seeking refuge within the country or abroad. Lebanon, due to its geographical proximity and historical ties, became one of the main destinations for Syrians escaping the civil war. Around 1.2 million Syrians have registered with the UNHCR in Lebanon.

Despite being a small country, slightly larger than Cyprus, with a population of about 4 million, Lebanon faced challenges in accommodating the large number of Syrian refugees. The country's political factions and paramilitary groups were closely involved in events in Syria, and Lebanese state institutions had limited capacity to provide essential services and security, even to Lebanese nationals.

Five years ago, there were concerns that the conflict in Syria might spill over into Lebanon. However, security incidents remained localized and episodic. While the refugee crisis raised concerns and was perceived as a destabilizing factor, its impact was not as disruptive as expected. Syrians in Lebanon faced vulnerability, especially those categorized as 'displaced' (nazih), who experienced increasing segregation.

A Glimpse Through Their Eyes

Summary:

Aya, Jameel, Fteim, Yasmin, and Mohamad, Syrian refugees in Lebanon, share their lives through the lens of a camera. In a country where life is becoming tougher, these individuals, among the 1.2 million Syrian refugees in Lebanon, receive EU-funded cash assistance as a vital support.

With 9 out of 10 refugee families in Lebanon living in extreme poverty, the assistance becomes a lifeline, helping them meet essential needs. The EU funds the World Food Program (WFP) to provide monthly cash transfers to the most vulnerable refugees. In July 2022 alone, WFP assisted over 37,000 Syrian households. The EU Trust Fund for Syria also supports vulnerable people in Lebanon with monthly cash assistance.

Here are some accounts of the Refugees:

1.   Aya's Struggle in Majdal Aanjar:
Aya, a 19-year-old from Damascus, lives in Majdal Aanjar with her family. Cash assistance has eased some pressure off the family, lifting them from a situation where they received no aid, and debts were piling up.

2.   Fteim's Tent in Bekaa Valley:
Fteim lives with her four children and husband in a tent in Bekaa Valley. Despite receiving cash assistance since 2019,

life is still a struggle, with cold winters, hot summers, and the need to purchase vegetables as food prices rise.

3.   Jameel's Strife in Bekaa:

Jameel, a father of three, resides in an informal tented settlement in Bekaa. Unemployed, cash assistance helps him pay off debts. His family's costs exceed the monthly transfer, limiting them to basic food items like rice, bulgur, and beans.

4.   Mohamad's Resilience and Small Garden:

Mohamad, who fled Homs at 11, works installing TV satellites. His family, receiving cash assistance from 2020, maintains a small vegetable garden on their balcony and raises chickens, ensuring a constant source of eggs and protein.

5.   Yasmin's Struggle in Majdal Aanjar:

Yasmin, a single mother with two children, fled Damascus in 2014. Living in Majdal Aanjar with her family, she has difficulty making ends meet. Cash assistance since 2021 has provided relief, reducing her dependence on her brothers for food, basic needs, and medication.

Educational Resilience: Layla as a Case-study

Facing financial issues could make going to school difficult.

Personal Account by Layla: Hey, I'm Layla, and I want to tell you about I not giving up on school even when things got really hard. This happens to a lot of us in Lebanon.

Money troubles made it super hard for me to stay in school. Paying for classes became a big problem, and it felt really heavy. I had to find a way, so I started working part-time jobs. Balancing work and school wasn't easy. Some days, I went to class without eating because I didn't have enough money.

One semester was especially tough. I had to work extra hours just to get by. It was tiring, and sometimes I thought about quitting. But giving up on school wasn't something I wanted to do.

I had a dream, and I knew school was the way to reach it. It wasn't just about getting a paper saying I finished; it was about making a better future for myself. And I held onto that dream really tight.

In Lebanon, many students like me were facing similar problems because the country was going through a hard time. We shared experiences about working odd jobs, struggling to buy books, and making hard choices to keep going to school. It wasn't easy, but we, the students, knew how important school was in our lives.

What kept me going was thinking that school is our hope. It's not just about tests and grades; it's about making a better life. We, the young people, stick to school because it's our way to move forward.

Yeah, it was tough. Sometimes I wondered if it was all worth it. But the dream of a better future, the idea that school is the key—that's what kept me going. And I know lots of others felt the same. We were not just students; we were dreamers, holding onto our hopes even when things were really hard.

Mental Health in Lebanon

The situation in Lebanon has made mental health a big issue. For more than 20 years, Shayma struggled with depression. She lives in Saida, a city in southern Lebanon that was hit hard by economic problems. Shayma found it difficult to get help for her mental health. While there are health centers, they are mostly focused on physical health, and not mental health. Shayma felt her psychological needs were ignored, and she did not know of any mental health services that were available.

Shayma, a 38-year-old mom of four, faced a tough upbringing. Abandoned by her parents, she grew up with strict grandparents. When she got married at 18, she hoped to escape, but her living conditions remained difficult. Seeking emotional relief, many in her community turned to a religious authority called a Cheikh. Shayma heard about psychological support sessions but faced a lot of stigma. Eventually, her struggles led her to seek therapy.

In 2013, after childbirth, Shayma had a breakdown. She resisted mental health care at first due to society's judgment but after years of struggle, she realized her mental health was more important than people's opinions. Organizations like Première Urgence International are working to integrate mental health services into primary healthcare. Shayma has been in therapy for about six months and believes there should be more awareness about mental health care.

The economic crisis, combined with stigma, makes accessing mental health care difficult. People's well-being is at risk, with rising mental health issues like depression and anxiety. Stigma, lack of awareness, and financial constraints, all limit access to care. The National Mental Health Program is trying to integrate mental health services into primary care, but the challenges remain.

Stigmatization of mental health is a global issue. The Première Urgence International MHPSS team reports a significant impact on social life and family cohesion due to the economic crisis. Daily struggles are affecting people's mental health, especially for vulnerable populations like refugees.

Première Urgence International [2] is supporting Lebanon's Ministry of Public Health in integrating mental health services. They train healthcare providers to offer psychological counseling. People like Shayma are finding

---

[2] https://www.premiere-urgence.org/en/break-the-stigma-lets-talk-about-mental-health-in-lebanon/

relief through therapy, and there's a growing need for more awareness about mental health in Lebanon.

In summary, the economic crisis in Lebanon has exacerbated mental health issues, and the stigma surrounding mental health care makes it challenging to access help. Organizations are working to integrate mental health services into primary care and raise awareness about the importance of mental well-being.

Holding on to hope during Lebanon's hardest times

A breeze comes through the windows in Nadine's living room in Beirut. It's a hot day, and the heatwave is finally easing up. Nadine, who is visually impaired, carefully moves around the room. She sits with her five-year-old daughter Joya, and they share a smile.

When asked about life in Lebanon, Nadine responds with a mix of sarcasm, despair, strength, and hope. "Absolutely lovely," she says.

Nadine, 44, lives with her husband and three children. Facing some tricky situations, the family has relied on aid for the past four years. The economic situation in Lebanon has been tough for everyone, and Nadine's family is no exception. The value of the Lebanese pound has drastically fallen, making it challenging for them to afford the basics.

"The problems in Lebanon started four years ago with the uprising [in 2019], followed by Covid-19, the currency crisis, and the Beirut port explosion," explains Nadine. "All these events happened one after the other, and we did not have time to catch our breath. These are all issues that are difficult to deal with.

"The situation wasn't like this before. There were challenges, but our income was sufficient. Now, even when there's a job, we're still struggling."

Nadine's story mirrors the struggles of many Lebanese families hit hard by the economic crisis. According to a recent study, around 3.9 million people in Lebanon need humanitarian assistance.

Nadine's home is her safe space. Being visually impaired, she finds it challenging to go out often. She has lived in the same house for four years, making it familiar and navigable.

"I can't leave the house frequently. [My home is] everything to me. I know every corner; I've adapted here."

However, housing and rent have become major concerns for Nadine. The economic crisis led to a significant increase in rent costs. Monthly rent, on average, jumped from 2,000,000 Lebanese pounds to 13,000,000 pounds. This made it tough for many families, including Nadine's, to cover the basics.

"I don't like when the landlord comes to my door asking for rent," says Nadine. "If I had the money, I wouldn't put off payments for three months."

Nadine received assistance from the Norwegian Refugee Council (NRC) shelter team, covering house rent for six months. This aid helped the family with other expenses, including food, amidst soaring inflation rates.

"The lease agreement with the organization [NRC] ended in May, and now the landlord wants to raise the rent and will only accept dollars. He is asking for $250 instead of the $150 we used to pay. If we cannot pay the rent, we'll have to leave, and he'll give us a two month notice to find a new home. But where do we go?"

While the assistance provided relief for six months, Nadine is aware that the situation remains challenging for many others. "Six months of rent coverage isn't enough. Many people still need help. I'm fortunate to have a roof over my head, but others don't. I could be homeless one day."

Nadine highlights the difficulty of affording essential items. The family relies on food donations and struggles to buy vegetables. The economic collapse in Lebanon, marked by skyrocketing inflation, has made it hard for people to afford even basic goods.

"We're living off food donations and have got used to it. We can't afford to buy vegetables. It's quite hard for us to afford tomatoes. Sometimes we get them during the school semester so that my children can go to school with a simple sandwich. This is the situation for everyone."

Nadine's health has also suffered due to malnutrition. She cannot afford healthcare and needs a blood transfusion, but the cost is prohibitive.

"I need a blood transfusion for treatment. I don't have health insurance, and going to the hospital would cost no less than a thousand dollars. This might be due to malnutrition since we don't eat healthy food. I have fainted several times."

Despite the challenges, Nadine and her husband are determined to provide education for their children. With the quality of public schools affected by frequent strikes, Nadine prefers not to enroll her children there. However, the family faces difficulties in covering the costs of private education.

"I only care about educating them. We are doing our best to ensure that our children learn. It's a lifesaver."

Nadine expresses hope for a better political situation in Lebanon, wishing for improvements for the sake of the next generation.

"I can't provide for my children because of the people ruling this country. The blame falls on all these political parties and corruption in the country," says Nadine. Despite all the difficulties, she and her husband remain determined to look forward with hope for their children.

Towards Rebuilding:

Lebanon endured a devastating explosion on August 4, 2020, causing widespread destruction in Beirut. The blast, resulting from the ignition of stored ammonium nitrate at the port, claimed over 200 lives and left around 6,000 injured. This tragic incident triggered protests, leading to the government's resignation a week later. Lebanon was already grappling with economic challenges and protests since 2019, driven by corruption and mismanagement.

The country's economic woes were deeply rooted, characterized by chronic corruption, significant debt, a devalued currency, and soaring inflation. Mass demonstrations in October 2019, initially peaceful, demanded a new government and an end to corruption. Despite changes in leadership, economic conditions worsened, exacerbated by the COVID-19 pandemic, which not only impacted public health but intensified the economic decline.

The catastrophic explosion added another layer of crisis, causing extensive damage and leaving many homeless. The aftermath led to protests and eventually the government's resignation. Lebanon's economy faced a severe contraction, described by the World Bank as one of the worst crises in the last 150 years. The Lebanese lira lost around 80% of its value against the US Dollar, and inflation soared. Basic necessities, including 80% of the country's food, became more expensive.

Concerns arose about food security, with estimates indicating that 75% of the population faced difficulties in putting food on the table. Lebanon, hosting 1.5 million refugees – the highest per capita in the world – experienced overwhelming challenges. International aid efforts were mobilized to address the aftermath of the explosion and the ongoing economic crisis. However, the path to recovery remained complex, requiring not only immediate relief but also long-term solutions to address systemic issues.

Amid these challenges, the education system suffered, with private schools struggling financially. Many students were expected to transfer to public schools. The Lebanese Evangelical School Tyre (LEST), emphasizing spiritual education, faced uncertainties. A fundraising project aimed to support students unable to afford fees, prioritizing those facing loss or special needs. This effort reflects a commitment to provide hope amid Lebanon's multifaceted crisis.

Prayers are also sought for peace, justice, and mercy for the country from time to time. Additionally, prayers are extended to those working to bring hope and make decisions at various levels. The Lebanese people face the daunting task of rebuilding their lives, and international support remains crucial in navigating these challenges.

Seeds of Change: Empowering the Youths

This project, called YOUth CAN!, is being run by the European Union in Lebanon. It started in March 2020 and continued until March 2022. The goal was to help young people in Lebanon, especially in the northern part of the country, find jobs and build sustainable businesses.

Lebanon is facing a serious unemployment problem, especially among young people. More than 35% of young people in Lebanon are unemployed, which is higher than the global average of 25%. This project focuses on the northern part of Lebanon, which has the highest youth unemployment rate.

Even having a university degree does not guarantee a job. The reasons for youth unemployment include economic and political instability, lack of job opportunities, and challenges in getting the right information and support for career guidance.

In recent years, there has been an effort to support young entrepreneurs in Lebanon, especially through start-ups. However, these efforts have been scattered, and many young business owners struggle to survive and grow. This project aims to change that by providing better support and opportunities for young people to access the job market.

The European Union is working on this project with a budget of €555,556, with €500,000 coming from the EU. The project is implemented in partnership with OXFAM Italy. The focus is not only on helping young entrepreneurs but also on making sure their voices are heard in policies and decision-making.

The practical information about the project is as follows:

- Overview: Multi-sector
- Budget: €555,556 (€500,000 from the EU)
- Location: Northern Lebanon
- Project Duration: March 2020 - March 2022
- Implementing Partner: OXFAM Italy

Other projects by the European Union in Lebanon include efforts to support children affected by armed conflict, promote youth empowerment for social impact, challenge stereotypes, support olive and beekeeping cooperatives, and more.

Questions

1. What is the main focus of Chapter 5 - Human Stories Amidst the Rubble?

2. How does the chapter present real stories of Lebanese individuals?

3. Can you provide examples of personal experiences during crises that are highlighted in this chapter?

4. In what ways does the chapter contribute to portraying the human side of the struggle faced by the Lebanese people?

5. Are there recurring themes or patterns in the human stories shared, and if so, what are they?

6. Does the chapter delve into the impact of external factors, such as wars or economic challenges on the lives of the individuals mentioned?

7. How is resilience and the ability to overcome adversity depicted in the human stories presented in this chapter?

8. Are there connections made between these human stories and broader themes like cultural identity or economic instability within Lebanon's narrative?

9. Does the chapter offer any reflections or lessons drawn from the personal experiences shared?

10. In what ways does the chapter contribute to a deeper understanding of the lived experiences of the Lebanese people during challenging times?

Chapter 6: Collapse of the Currency

Now, when we say, "currency collapse," we mean that the Lebanese currency, known as the pound, was devalued. It is like owning a Mercedes vehicle that was worth 100.000.00 dollars yesterday, and today it is only worth 1000.00 dollars The currency collapse caused severe issues for the people of Lebanon and impacted the lives of many.

Why did this happen, you may want to ask? Well, there were multiple reasons. Lebanon has been dealing with unethical leaders and a shaky political situation. On top of that, the country was in debt, and things were not going well economically. These issues caused the currency to plummet.

So, how did all of this affect the people of Lebanon? Let us break it down.

First, basic products became more expensive. Imagine that you wake up one day and food, products, and services tripled in price. That is exactly what happened in Lebanon – prices inflated to a degree that it became difficult for families to purchase everyday necessities.

Next, people's savings were lost in banks and salaries earned for work were not enough anymore. This is what many people in Lebanon faced – their money was not as powerful as before, and it made life extremely difficult.

Even having a job became tricky. Many businesses had to shut down due to the monetary crisis. This meant that many people lost their jobs, making it even more difficult for families to purchase necessities.

Now, let us discuss how the people of Lebanon dealt with all these challenges.

Some folks got creative. They started finding new ways to earn money, like starting small businesses or working online. It is similar to figuring out a new game or puzzle – you keep trying until something works.

People also came together to help each other out. Look at it this way, it is as if your neighbor shared their food with you because they knew your family was struggling and that is what happened in Lebanon – communities formed groups to support each other. They shared meals and helped those who were struggling.

Understanding the Currency Collapse:

The country's currency, called the Lebanese pound, decreased in value compared to the US dollar. This was a huge issue that the Lebanese people had to deal with. In 2019, 1,500 Lebanese pounds were equal to 1 US dollar, but now it is

100,000 Lebanese pounds for 1 US dollar. This economic crisis made life extremely difficult for the people of Lebanon, pushing many Lebanese citizens into poverty.

The political leaders in Lebanon, who are responsible for the country's financial issues, have not been able to fix the currency's collapse. The situation in Lebanon became so difficult that many banks in Lebanon had to shut down and close their doors due to disagreements and issues with people attempting to withdraw their funds.

Despite these challenges, the people of Lebanon are doing their best to cope with the situation. Some started small businesses, and communities are supporting those in need. However, the lack of action from political leaders and ongoing economic problems makes it difficult for the average citizen in Lebanon.

Factors Contributing to the Collapse:

The collapse of the Lebanese pound was an unavoidable crisis, and some of the reasons for the collapse include, chronic corruption, which translates to people in power behaving unethically for long periods of time. Also, there is mismanagement, which is not handling finances professionally and ethically. Lebanon's weak government complicates the situation further.

Now, think of the country owing a lot of debt, this, along with an unstable economy, is the perfect recipe for disaster. It made the country's currency, the Lebanese pound, fall very quickly. So, corruption, mismanagement, and a shaky political scene mixed with debt and economic issues all together led to this unstable situation.

Economic Repercussions on Citizens:

Soaring Inflation:

In January of 2022, prices in Lebanon skyrocketed – by about 124 percent. This meant products and services became much more expensive. This happened due to the country's economic and financial crisis. For example, prices skyrocketed, and everything including communication, education, health, and the cost of staying in hotels and eating at restaurants started increasing. Even the costs of basic needs like food, water, shelter, and energy increased tremendously.

The Central Administration of Statistics' Consumer Price Index, which reflects the standard cost of goods, increased by about 8.43 percent from December 2022. Experts' claim that the situation in Lebanon is difficult due to Lebanon's economy being unstable for years. The value of the country's currency, the Lebanese pound, has dropped and lost 90 percent of its value in February of 2019.

In 2021, prices went up by 155 percent, and in 2022, they went up by 171.2 percent – the highest in about 40 years. Imagine paying one dollar for an item in 2021 and having to pay more than two and a half dollars for the same item in 2022.

Specifically, costs for communication increased by a massive 331 percent in January of 2023 when compared to January of 2022. Other things like education, health, and staying in hotels or eating out became expensive too, by 191 percent, 176 percent, and 174 percent, respectively.

The costs of water, electricity, gas, and diesel went up by 163 percent every year. Prices for clothing, food and drinks also increased by 161 percent and 138 percent, respectively.

Compared to December 2022, the costs of goods that people purchase for everyday use went up by 20 percent, and staying in hotels or eating at restaurants became 18 percent more expensive.

Healthcare treatment, costs of food, non-alcoholic drinks, water, electricity, gas, and other fuels increased by 11 percent.

Lebanon's economy declined by roughly 58 percent between 2019 and 2021. This was a massive drop. The total value of the Gross Domestic Product (GDP) went from $52 billion in 2019 to only $21.8 billion in 2021, according to the World Bank. This is one of the greatest declines in history!

To make things worse, the tax revenue declined by more than half between 2019 and 2021 due to Lebanon's economic crisis.

The International Monetary Fund (IMF), which supports countries that are experiencing financial trouble, stated that Lebanon's tax system must be fixed, or the country will keep losing money. The Lebanese tax system which also includes customs and other fees, is not working properly and this caused Lebanon to lose around 4.8 percent of its GDP in 2022.

The World Bank, which is an international financial institution that provides loans and grants to the governments of low- and middle-income countries for the purpose of pursuing capital projects states that Lebanon is going through one of the worst financial situations in history. The difficult situation has made more than half of the Lebanese people live below the poverty line, and many Lebanese citizens have immigrated in pursuit of a better life.

The leaders of Lebanon have not implemented the required changes that are needed in order to revive the economy. There is an estimated 3 billion dollars of support funds from the IMF, and another 11 billion dollars promised by other countries, however, the support funds will only be disbursed once Lebanon's leaders work together, form a new government, and implement important changes. The problem is that the Lebanese politicians disagree on certain issues and have not been able to reach any resolutions. As of 2024 Lebanon does not have a president and it has been nine months since the last attempt for Lebanese elections occurred. The country has not yet formed a new government. The situation is difficult for the people of Lebanon, and there is a lot of uncertainty when thinking about the future.

Unemployment Crisis:

Most Lebanese households rely on support from their family members who are living abroad, making Lebanon a "rentier economy." Sadly, the leaders of Lebanon did not focus on creating new jobs within the country. Instead, they made many people choose to work abroad and immigrate.

The leaders of Lebanon did not invest in creating new industries or farming; instead, they concentrated on banking and tourism. This led to a weak economy.

To fix the high unemployment rate, Lebanon needs to rebuild its financial structure and economic system. Political changes are crucial for Lebanon.

The country spent huge amounts of money on education, however, this did not resolve any issues as many graduates were unable to find jobs following graduation. Lebanon also had more skilled workers than needed, the supply for skilled labor was greater than the demand.

The economic collapse also affected education. Public schools and Lebanese Universities struggled due to the lack of support from the government. This made education in Lebanon a luxury that only the ultra-rich enjoyed. The government supported private educational institutions, leaving public schools with very little to no support.

To solve Lebanon's unemployment crisis, a political solution is necessary. The Lebanese youth should take part of the decision-making process because they understand the issues and are able to find resolutions. Operating under a government of experts, outside of the usual political system, is crucial. Gender balance is also important.

A proposed new plan must be put in place, with the guidance of the International Monetary Fund (IMF) focusing on changing the Lebanese Lira's value, restructuring the financial system, and making other necessary improvements. This could potentially shift Lebanon's economy from being dependent on banking and tourism to more productive sectors such as agriculture and industry.

Lebanon has the potential to become a hub for technology companies. A stronger focus on agriculture can create more jobs and boost the economy. The government must support local industries, encourage foreign investments, and balance funding between agriculture, industry, and other sectors.

In conclusion, solving Lebanon's unemployment crisis requires both political and economic changes. It is time for the Lebanese youth to take part of the decision-making process and for Lebanon to focus on a better future for its citizens.

Coping Strategies and Survival Stories:

Diversification of Income Sources:

Lebanon has not invested enough in transportation, electricity, and digital connections. These shortcomings in infrastructure make it difficult for Lebanon to diversify its economy. Many of Lebanon's businesses operate informally, not following regulations and avoiding taxes. This does not help the government and these practices make it difficult for businesses to compete fairly.

Lebanon's education system also needs improvement to prepare people for a more varied job market. An improved educational system could potentially support the workforce and help employees take advantage of various job opportunities. Diversifying the economy has many potential benefits which include making Lebanon less sensitive to economic issues. This could also create more jobs, specifically for the youth of Lebanon. Rather than relying on tourism for an economic boost, a more diverse economy could grow steadily over time creating more opportunities for the Lebanese people.

In order to diversify, Lebanon first needs to fix its political issues and the corruption that exists. We also need a better infrastructure and more regulations for businesses. Encouraging entrepreneurship and innovation, while supporting small businesses could help diversify economic activities. Supporting small businesses with financial incentives and programs is crucial. Also, an improved digital infrastructure could encourage e-commerce and tech-based industries to grow in Lebanon.

In conclusion, Lebanon must diversify its economy in order to have a stable and prosperous future. This may be difficult, however, the benefits such as stability, job creation, and long-term growth, are worth the effort. Something like this would require the government, businesses, and society to work together.

The people of Lebanon are exploring various ways to diversify their income sources due to economic challenges and uncertainties in the country. Some common strategies include:

1.   **Freelancing and Online Work:**
- Many Lebanese individuals are turning to freelancing opportunities and online work. This includes jobs in fields like writing, graphic design, programming, and digital marketing.
- Online platforms and freelancing websites allow Lebanese professionals to offer their services globally, expanding their client base and income streams.

2.   **E-commerce and Online Businesses:**
- Entrepreneurs are venturing into e-commerce by selling products online. This could involve creating handmade crafts, art, or even launching small-scale online stores for local products.
- The rise of social media has also enabled individuals to market and sell products directly to consumers.

3.   **Investments and Trading:**
- Some Lebanese people are exploring investment opportunities in financial markets, real estate, or

cryptocurrencies. Investing in stocks or mutual funds can provide additional income if done wisely.

- Trading activities, such as buying and selling stocks or engaging in forex trading, are becoming avenues for potential income generation.

4.   Tech and Innovation:

- Individuals with tech skills are developing innovative solutions, apps, or software that can be monetized. This could involve creating mobile applications, software tools, or providing tech-related services.

- Tech entrepreneurship is gaining traction, especially among the younger generation.

5.   Real Estate Ventures:

- Despite challenges in the real estate sector, some Lebanese individuals are exploring opportunities in property development, rental properties, or real estate investment trusts (REITs).

- Renting out properties or investing in real estate projects can provide a steady income stream.

6.   Consulting and Advisory Services:

- Professionals in various fields, such as finance, law, or marketing, are offering consulting services. This involves providing expert advice to businesses or individuals for a fee.

- Consulting can be done independently or through joining consulting firms.

7. **Agriculture and Farming:**

- Some Lebanese people are returning to traditional sectors like agriculture and farming. Cultivating and selling agricultural products or engaging in agribusiness can diversify income sources.

- This also aligns with the growing interest in sustainable and locally sourced products.

8. **Educational Services:**

- Given the importance of education, offering tutoring, language classes, or skill development courses is a way some Lebanese individuals are supplementing their income.

- Online platforms facilitate reaching a broader audience for educational services.

9. **Tourism and Hospitality Ventures:**

- Despite challenges in the tourism sector, individuals are exploring niche opportunities in hospitality. This could involve opening small guesthouses, providing unique travel experiences, or catering services.

- Catering to local tourism can provide income while contributing to the recovery of the sector.

10. **Collaborative Initiatives and Partnerships:**

- Collaborative efforts and partnerships among individuals with complementary skills or businesses are becoming more common. This allows for shared resources, risks, and benefits.

11.   Community Support Networks:

Lebanese communities have come together in order to support one another. Many have started community kitchens, where neighbors shared meals to make sure everyone had enough to eat. These community kitchens were a way to fight against the problem of not having enough food, which is called food insecurity.

There were also groups called mutual aid networks. These networks provided support to those who were in need. If someone was going through difficult times or facing challenges, mutual aid networks were there to lend a helping hand.

These community initiatives were like a safety net for people, making sure nobody was left behind or struggling alone.

In other words, people in Lebanon became one big family. They shared food, helped each other out, and made sure nobody felt alone.

Organizations that have continued to help the people of Lebanon till date:[3]

---

[3] https://beunsettled.co/blog/7-ways-we-can-help-our-community-in-beirut/

A.　　Impact Lebanon: This is a local group that helps during difficult circumstances. They are working with other groups who need help right away.

B.　　Lebanese Red Cross: These are the people who help when someone is hurt or sick. They need more money to reach more people.

C.　　Beit El Baraka: This group helps older people in Lebanon who are having a hard time due to price inflation.

D.　　Baytna Baytak (Housing Help): Funds given here helps find places for people to stay if their homes are destroyed.

E.　　Just Help - Lebanon Relief Fund: This money is for medicine, rebuilding, and food for families who need it.

F.　　Help Lebanon: This is a way to give money to groups and hospitals.

G.　　Your Heart and Mind: Even if we are far away, we can still care about Lebanon and its people. We need to remember that Lebanon is more than just this sad time.

Bonus groups that are also good to support:

- Donner Sans Computer: This group helps with blood donations to save lives.
- Beautiful People - Lebanon: They make food for families who do not have enough.
- Lebanese Food Bank: This group gives food to people who need it.

Questions

1.   Can you provide an overview of the in-depth analysis presented regarding the currency collapse?

2.   How does the chapter explore the economic repercussions of the currency collapse on Lebanese citizens?

3.   Are coping strategies and survival stories highlighted in this chapter? If so, what are some examples?

4.   Does the chapter discuss the factors or events that led to the collapse of the currency, providing historical context?

5.   In what ways does the chapter contribute to a better understanding of the impact of economic challenges on the daily lives of Lebanese citizens?

6.   Are there insights into how the collapse of the currency affected different sectors of society, such as businesses, households, or specific demographics?

7.   How do personal stories within the chapter reflect the broader economic situation in Lebanon during the currency collapse?

8.   Does the chapter offer any reflections on potential solutions or strategies to address the economic challenges discussed?

9.   In summary, what are the key takeaways from Chapter 6 in relation to the collapse of the currency in Lebanon?

Chapter 7: Struggle and Resilience

When difficult times hit, the Lebanese people have shown incredible strength and resilience.

Lebanon, a country with a lot of history, diversity and different cultures, has been through extremely difficult times. From monetary troubles to problems with the government and, most recently, a big explosion in Beirut. However, regardless of all these difficulties, the people of Lebanon never gave up, and always worked hard to rebuild.

Looking at how the people of Lebanon deal with ongoing difficulties shows us strength, faith, and resilience. One big way is by helping each other out.

The Lebanese people also have their own way of handling difficulties, they stick together as one big family and they find comfort in their culture and art. Lebanon's rich culture becomes a source of strength, helping people connect with their roots and giving them inspiration to face problems.

When facing difficulties, Lebanese communities show incredible strength. They begin rebuilding destroyed homes immediately after a tragedy occurs and they also start projects that support the locals.

Zooming in, we hear of stories that require personal strength. Entrepreneurs start their businesses again, families rebuild their homes from scratch, and students continue their education. These stories show the unbeatable spirit of the Lebanese people.

During difficult times, the Lebanese people draw from their inner strength and determination. They do not allow difficult times to define them. Finding hope when things seem impossible and rebuilding what was damaged shows an unmatched resilience.

Resilient Communities:

Lebanese people often help each other in small and quiet ways. Families, friends, and neighbors support each other, especially during hard times.

People in Lebanon believe in taking care of their friends and family first. They often mention religious teachings about loving your neighbor. While it is true that communities in Lebanon are often divided by religion, the idea of helping those close to you goes beyond religious lines.

Even though Lebanon can be a bit segregated, with different religious groups living in different areas, people still help each other regardless of their background. Sometimes, living in the same building or neighborhood is enough of a reason to lend a hand. People help each other with money, electricity, or even just offering support to the building caretaker.

Unlike big institutions, neighbors, teachers, family, and friends can spot when someone is struggling. This closeness is crucial because many people do not want to ask for help openly. For example, someone might not admit they need help to buy food, but a friend or neighbor who knows them well can offer assistance quietly.

This personal knowledge helps create a sense of trust. People are more willing to help when they know it makes a real difference. People prefer giving through informal channels, like helping a neighbor directly, rather than going through big organizations.

In Lebanon it is not about the rich helping the poor, even middle-class and lower-class families find ways to help. The economic struggles affect everyone regardless of their social class. Charitable organizations and political figures often help in a way that feels distant or condescending.

Interestingly, the Lebanese diaspora, people who left Lebanon and decided to reside abroad, also contribute financially. They provide scholarships and raise funds to support people back home. This type of support feels more genuine and direct when compared to support from wealthy individuals.

Lebanon also faces challenges due to wealth being concentrated at the top. Wealth is not redistributed evenly. Lebanese people rely on informal networks to get by. For example, local shops let customers buy items on credit. The small lines of credit, often interest-free, are part of the many ways families cope with tough times.

Lebanon might look like a middle-income country from the outside, but many people work multiple jobs, borrow money, and use improvised safety nets just to make ends meet. This resilience is not some magical power but rather a result of practical tactics that the Lebanese people use to navigate through difficult circumstances.

Lebanon is a country with contradictions. While the political system often highlights differences and competition, at the grassroots level, people show generosity, empathy, and a strong sense of community. What keeps the country together is not the political truce, but the way the Lebanese people support each other.

Individual Resilience:

Lebanon's economic troubles stem from years of financial mismanagement. Government decisions, along with actions by banks and the central bank, depleted foreign currency reserves. This led to an 80% devaluation of the Lebanese pound, causing people to lose their life savings overnight. Prices of essential goods have surged, making life incredibly difficult.

Lebanon heavily relies on services, importing much of what it consumes. With the plummeting currency value and a shortage of dollars, many businesses struggle to stay open. Even salaries, if not slashed outright, have lost their purchasing power. The once vibrant tourism sector has also suffered due to political and economic instability.

The impact is staggering. Numerous restaurants have closed, and thousands have lost jobs in the restaurant sector alone. Remittances, a vital income source, have declined, contributing to the economic downturn. This has caused a significant portion of the middle class, around 65% of the population, to fall into poverty.

In response to the government's inability to address these challenges, people are resorting to unconventional means. Barter groups on Facebook have emerged, where individuals exchange items desperately needed for daily survival. The desperation has led to shocking incidents, like someone holding up a pharmacy for diapers or resorting to robbery to feed their family.

While mass protests in 2019 led to the downfall of the government, the new administration has failed to improve living conditions. Misery is evident in closed shops, disrupted services, and frequent power cuts lasting up to 20 hours a day.

The myth of Lebanese resilience, often depicted in stories of dancing through hardships, has been shattered. The real resilience lies with politicians who refuse to step down despite plunging the country into bankruptcy. Even Lebanese banks, once considered resilient, are now under scrutiny for their role in the crisis.

The International Monetary Fund's attempts to intervene face resistance from banks unwilling to undergo necessary financial audits. Meanwhile, resignations of high-ranking officials reveal corruption, with billions smuggled abroad while small depositors face restrictions.

The situation is dire. Organizations like Ashkal Alwan, supporting local arts, have faced funding seizures, disrupting their decades-long contributions. Exhaustion and despair permeate the country as dreams of a better future fade away.

Lebanon's struggle exposes the harsh reality: resilience is not a magical quality but a coping mechanism in the face of ongoing challenges. The myth of resilience, once a source of pride, now serves as a painful reminder of the failures of the state and its leaders. As the Lebanese people reject this myth, they confront the harsh conditions that necessitated its creation in the first place. Despite the despair, there is a ray of optimism as the realization dawns that a myth, no matter how appealing, cannot replace a life half-lived.

Lessons for the World:

Lebanon's story is like a guide for everyone, teaching important lessons about dealing with tough times. It shows us how communities become stronger by helping each other, the impact of holding onto your cultural identity, and how resilience can grow even during challenging situations.

In our connected world, learning from the experiences of the Lebanese people can inspire everyone to face their challenges together.

Lebanon has been through many wars and conflicts. When times are tough, communities come together to help by sharing resources, offering shelter, or just saying kind words. This is a reminder for the whole world that when we face challenges, helping each other out can make a big difference.

Lebanon is a place full of history and diverse cultures. Even with many difficulties, the Lebanese people hold onto their cultural identity. This teaches us that knowing who you are and where you come from can be a source of strength. Even in tough times, embracing your cultural roots can give you a sense of belonging and pride. For the world, this is a lesson about celebrating our differences and understanding that diversity makes us stronger.

Lebanon's journey shows us that resilience and the ability to bounce back from difficult situations, is a powerful force. No matter how difficult a situation may become, the people of Lebanon will find a way to keep going. It is a reminder for all of us that even when facing big challenges, we can find strength within ourselves and our communities to overcome those challenges. Resilience is like a muscle that grows stronger with every difficulty, and Lebanon's experience can inspire the world to keep pushing forward.

In today's world, where countries and people are more connected than ever, Lebanon's lessons become even more important. The struggles and triumphs of the Lebanese people can inspire a global community to face challenges together. When we understand and appreciate each other's stories, this creates a sense of unity that can help us solve shared problems like climate change, health crises, and social inequalities. Lebanon teaches us that a united world can find solutions to complex issues.

The Lebanon experience is a light to the world, showing that even in the face of huge challenges, a community can stand strong, celebrate its identity, and bounce back with resilience. As the world faces its own difficulties, these lessons from Lebanon can guide us towards a future where unity, cultural pride, and mutual support lead the way.

Questions

1.   How does the chapter examine the endurance of the Lebanese people in the face of ongoing challenges?

2.   In what ways does the chapter explore how individuals cope with the various difficulties presented in Lebanon's narrative?

3.   Does the chapter provide insights into the factors or qualities that contribute to the resilience of Lebanese communities and individuals?

4. How does the chapter contribute to a deeper understanding of the psychological and social aspects of resilience within the Lebanese context?

5. Are there any connections made between the personal stories of resilience and broader societal impacts in Lebanon?

6. In what ways does the chapter inspire or offer lessons for readers in building resilience in their own lives or communities?

7. Can you summarize the key messages or takeaways from Chapter 7 regarding the struggle and resilience of the Lebanese people?

Conclusion

As we wrap up our exploration of Lebanon's remarkable journey, the resounding theme of resilience permeates each chapter, underscoring the spirit of its people in the middle of its wars, conflicts, and daunting challenges.

Lebanon's strength comes from its communities standing together. When tough times come, people help each other by sharing things, giving a place to stay, and offering comfort. This support not only helps individuals but creates a strong community that can handle difficult situations.

Despite many issues, the Lebanese people stick to their cultural roots. In our connected world, learning to appreciate different cultures and celebrating diversity are important lessons.

Resilience, a recurring motif in Lebanon's narrative, transcends individual strength to become a collective force emanating from communities and the nation as a whole. In the face of adversities—wars, conflicts, or economic crises—Lebanon exemplifies the human spirit's capacity to endure and emerge stronger. Resilience, as Lebanon teaches us, is not the absence of challenges but the courage to confront them and persist.

In today's interconnected global landscape, Lebanon's lessons resonate more profoundly than ever. The struggles and triumphs of the Lebanese people offer a universal narrative that inspires a sense of unity. Understanding and appreciating each other's stories create bonds that transcend geographical boundaries. Lebanon becomes a guiding beacon, pointing the way toward collaborative solutions for shared global challenges like climate change, health crises, and social inequalities.

Reflecting on Lebanon's journey reveals that this narrative is not merely a historical account; it is a guide for the future. The lessons learned—emphasizing the importance of community, cultural pride, and resilience—serve as the foundational blocks for a more united world. Applying these principles globally equips us to navigate the complex challenges that lie ahead.

Resilience is not just a passive quality; it is an active response to adversity. Lebanon's ability to persist amid considerable challenges underscores the potency of this attribute. From the early days of conflict to more recent struggles, Lebanon's story depicts a nation repeatedly tested yet refusing to be defined by its hardships.

Crucially, resilience is not a solitary endeavor; it thrives in the collective determination of individuals, communities, and nations. Lebanon's story extends an invitation to the world: embrace the spirit of resilience, fostering an environment where challenges metamorphose into opportunities for growth and unity.

As we absorb the invaluable lessons from Lebanon, it's paramount to move beyond mere awareness. The global community holds a pivotal role in supporting nations that have faced profound challenges, with Lebanon standing as a testament to resilience. Acknowledgment must transition into active support, be it through humanitarian aid, diplomatic efforts, or collaborative initiatives. Standing in solidarity with nations like

Lebanon allows the global community to contribute not only to rebuilding efforts but also to the collective spirit of resilience.

In our rapidly flowing world of information, we possess the capacity to unite behind causes that promote unity, peace, and recovery. Lebanon's experience becomes a shared story, urging individuals, communities, and nations to act collectively for a brighter future.

As we conclude this comprehensive exploration of Lebanon's journey, we're left with a profound appreciation for the strength embedded in resilience. The chapters unfolded a narrative that traverses time, showcasing the endurance of a nation and its people.

Lebanon's story isn't confined to its past; it stands as a living testament to the power of resilience in shaping the present and guiding the future. In our interconnected and interdependent world, we can draw inspiration from Lebanon's lessons. By embracing community support, celebrating cultural identity, and nurturing resilience, we pave the way for a global narrative of unity and strength.

Let Lebanon's journey resonate as a call for collective action, a call to foster a world where shared challenges are met with shared determination. In unity, understanding, and support lies the path to a future where resilience is not merely a response but a prevailing force lighting the way forward.

Sources

Book Sources

Pity the Nation: The Abduction of Lebanon by Robert Fisk

Lebanon: A Country in Fragments by Andrew Arsan

Lebanon: A History, 600-2011 by William Harris

Website Sources

https://www.premiere-urgence.org/en/break-the-stigma-lets-talk-about-mental-health-in-lebanon/

https://www.aljazeera.com/features/2020/8/21/i-lost-everything-i-did-in-my-life-beirut-explosion-aftermath

https://civil-protection-humanitarian-aid.ec.europa.eu/news-stories/stories/through-their-own-lens-syrian-refugees-lebanon_en

https://www.echoesinternational.org.uk/rebuilding-hope/

https://www.eeas.europa.eu/delegations/lebanon/youth-can-promoting-youth-economic-empowerment-lebanon_en https://www.arab-reform.net/publication/lebanons-unemployment-crisis-strategies-for-job-creation-in-a-collapsed-economy/#:~:text=Moreover%2C%20unemployment%20rates%20are%20notably,within%20the%20Lebanese%20labor%20force.

About the Author

Ali R. Jaber (born April 7, 1993), popularly known as Pride of Lebanon, is a Lebanese American author, writer and motivational speaker based in Michigan, the United States. Born in Toledo, Ohio, the United States, the Jaber family originated in Nabatieh, Southern Lebanon. Jaber studied at Henry Ford College majoring in business administration and digital marketing. He is also a student at the University of Michigan Dearborn and has been a member of The National Society of Leadership and Success and Phi Theta Kappa Honor Society. Jaber is the author and writer of the books "Public Speaking: Motivational Speeches in Depth." and "Lebanon: A Chronicle of Resilience."

www.ingramcontent.com/pod-product-compliance
Lightning Source LLC
Chambersburg PA
CBRC090744110726
48005CB00007B/960